Go Get Your Go

LaTrivia Grady

Contents

INTRODUCTION

It's so easy in life to get to a place where things aren't bad, but they aren't really good either. Life happens. Days go by, then weeks, and before you know it, years have passed and things are still the same. We become comfortable living in a situation that is less than. We tell ourselves so many times that it's okay—that it's no big deal. But deep inside of our hearts, we know that there is more. We know that we were meant for more. We know that we can achieve more. The question is, are we ready today to succeed, to step out? Are we going to continue to remain comfortable and making excuses? Or is now your time to go get your "Go".

I Got My Go!

Today, I'm so excited about the life that I live. So many things in my life were chaotic for so many years. And yet now, I've lost the weight that I wanted to lose. I fixed my credit. I changed up my career so that I was doing what I wanted, because I had never gone after it before. I work in the corporate hospitality industry, but in addition to that, I've started my own staffing company. Instead of living for so many years like I did with the crazy hours, the inconsistent pay, I now understand that making that move to corporate and advancing has helped me live a more reliable, more consistent life. And from that, I've been able to build my staffing company. I help people find work and I get to be a go-to business for the folks in my area looking for temporary staffing. I'm still currently working in the corporate arena, but as

I'm doing it, I'm building this bigger dream that I had for myself. And every day when I get up, I look in the mirror and I say to myself, "Girl, go get your go."

Rescue Me

You see, for so many years I lived waiting for my knight in shining armor to show up and rescue me. But what I realized is that I had to be my own knight. I needed to save myself. Things can feel really bleak. You can so easily look at yourself in the mirror and not realize who you are. Not because you are not still that person you've always been, but just simply

because of the fact that you are not

going for it like you used to, or like

you know that you can.

It's Up To Me

My staffing company, I named it, 'We Get It Right'. I serve the niche market in Nashville, helping catering companies, hotels, and restaurant and event logistics companies to help them staff their events. It gives me such a good feeling to be able to provide work for people looking for a job and it provides me freedom and options to go where I want to and do what I want to do. Options that I didn't even think were possible, I have now. We have to change in order to get our "Go". We have to hold onto our power. To never give up the power that is within us to move onto our next. No longer am I living paycheck to paycheck. But rather now I can go on trips and live financially free. When it came to write this book, I was able to just write a check for it, as opposed to hoping that I had enough balance on my credit card and that I could make the minimum payment. It's a goal that I've always had, and I was able to achieve it. I can't even begin to tell you how wonderful that feels. Because now more than anything else, I know I can depend on me.

Finding Peace Within

I am so proud of where I am now, but I wasn't always successful. I wasn't always in control of my life, and living a life that I love. I was at a standpoint in my life before, and I had to realize that I needed to 'get my go' in order to get out of the rut that I was in. I had to file bankruptcy. I had a divorce. I was at the same job for the last 10 years, and I just realized that I was on a treadmill moving and it looked like I was getting some headway, but I was just running in the same spot. In doing this for years, I just finally got to the point where I said, "Okay, something's got to give." I needed to change something, and in order for me to change something, I needed to go get it, whatever that would be. At the time, it was several different things I needed. It was me trying to lose weight. It was me trying to fix my credit. It was me trying to change my career. It was me trying to just get out the rut and survive.

Where I was living comfortable and compromised, my world was spiraling out of my control. My marriage was ending. There was a time when I thought I needed this knight and shining armor. I thought I needed him to be everything for me. I'm divorced from that man now, and it became so clear that I had to be my own knight in shining armor. Each day I wake up and I realize that it was me, and that I needed to save myself. I have a proud moment every day when I look in the mirror now, because I realize that I had it in me the whole time. I just needed to get my "Go" and I needed to be consistent in whatever goals or dreams that I had. In order for me to obtain those, I needed to keep going and that in itself was a 10 year process. I don't want it to take you 10 years to find that peace. I want you to have it now.

We Bring It On Ourselves

My bills were overwhelming. Originally I filed a Chapter 13, only to later have to convert over to a Chapter 7. In a Chapter 13 bankruptcy, you keep your assets, but the courts determine how much you have to pay of your debts, and how long you have to do it. In a Chapter 7, your debts are wiped clean, but you usually have to give up all assets that can be sold and the money given to your creditors. I thought I could do it quietly and privately and that nobody else would know. I am honestly such a private person. Instead, I found out that the court system actually takes the payments out of your check and tells your employer all about it. I was in a place after filing bankruptcy where I just felt broken and lost. I had nowhere to live, so I needed to rent an apartment. The bankruptcy was a glaring red mark on my credit, so I had to have a friend co-sign just so I could have a place to live. I had lost my house throughout the course of the divorce. I was in a situation that I should not have been in. It was based on the decisions that I had made to put me here. Sometimes the negativity we experience is something that we bring on ourselves.

Rebuilding

I remember the day I had discovered
that I was going to have to change
over from a Chapter 13 to Chapter 7.
In doing that, I was going to have to
have to walk away from my house.
We had bought the house, my ex-
husband and I, both having incomes,
not based on me doing it alone, and
now I was realizing that I wasn't

going to be able to afford the house by myself. It was so devastating. My ex didn't want the divorce and he didn't want to sell the house. I was living in the house. I was trying to maintain the house. I felt like a hostage to a house that I could not afford on one income. I was finally able to resolve things, but it meant I had to file Chapter 7. I had to sign over all of my rights to the house to my ex in order for me to walk away from the house and marriage. In a sense, we both won because he got the house and I was able to get the divorce to be free. I was broken, worried, feeling so ashamed of all that I had gone through. I sat there thinking and feeling, but then I realized that there was more in me.

That was 2013 when I had filed the bankruptcy, but what I discovered was that 2014 became the beginning of rebuilding my life. I learned that you always have options. Sometimes those options aren't always ideal, but we always have options, and those options give us freedom. What we have to do is look at what opportunities we do have, set a game plan and then go after it. You see, success is something intentional. It doesn't happen on accident. It doesn't happen if we are just sitting and waiting for it. To be successful, you have to have goals. You have to have a game plan and a way that you are going to reach those goals. I had to do this for every area of my being. Yes, financially, but also spiritually and emotionally and physically. I had to break them all down, see where I was, know where I wanted to be and then create a plan. After that, then I could move forward. That's when I looked myself in the mirror and I said, "Go get your go."

Asking the Hard Questions

It's something you can do too. Take a

long hard look at yourself today.

Wherever you are is not a place to

condemn yourself to, it just is a reality

of where you are right now. Get the

full picture of where you are right

now, but then begin to discover

where it is you are going, what you

need your "Go" for and how you are

going to get there. Ask yourself the questions:

1. What do I want?
2. What do I lack?
3. What are the things that I need?
4. What's my goal?
5. What is the game plan to get me to that goal?

We have to ask ourselves the hard questions. What do you need to be the best version of yourself? And then we have to live it out. This is a daily process. This isn't something that you just make a resolution on in January and expect it to all come together. You have to work it every day. There are no days off. Day by day, step by step. As you embrace the full picture of who you are and where you are going, you can go get it. You can live empowered. It's up to you.

Get Up And Move

Listen, I let myself get to the point that I did. We all let ourselves get to where we are. I had everything—who I am now—I had it in me then. I got comfortable and I didn't do the things that I needed to do then. I'm doing it now. Don't pause, get up and move. Get up and get your "Go." You are not going to get your "Go" standing still.

That standing still, that pause mode, you can't move forward just standing there. You have to go forward. You have to go get your "Go". I didn't believe in myself enough to move forward and keep going. Learn from my paused life. If you are standing there, you are wasting time. You are not moving.

Don't give up. Don't settle. But also, don't make excuses. Realize that you can do better. You have to stop looking like I was, for your knight in shining armor and discover the knight in shining armor that's always been there for you. That is you. We make the decision every day. We can decide to be comfortable. Or we can decide to be the best version of ourselves. Because the best you is something that you work at every day, you do it with the actions that you take, with the likeminded people that you surround yourself with, so you can have the support and encouragement and yes, the accountability to reach the goals that you've planned. I know what it's like. I know how easy it is to live where you are and to not go get your "Go". I lived there for many years. I was so comfortable. I let myself get to the point that I was financially, physically, and spiritually comfortable.

What I also know is that the person that I am now, I had in me all along. I just simply wasn't doing what I need to do before. I was living my life on pause. I wish I could go back and tell myself, "Don't pause your life, get up and move. Go get your go. You are not going to move forward by standing still. Girl, move your butt!" It's easy to get comfortable standing there. You can begin convincing yourself that you are not enough, to not believe in you and to begin to waste time in things that won't serve you. Not only the comfortability, but all of the cruel things that we say to ourselves when we are living in this place where we are not going for it. If I had done what I'm doing now, 10 years ago, I can't even imagine what my life would be like now.

I didn't simply take courage, step up and move forward. I let myself pause and stay still. Some of it was because I was comfortable. Some of it was because I was in an industry where most people don't stick around for a long time. And the fact that I had been there for so long, meant something. It was something I could do without thinking. It was repetitive. It was easy. It was comfortable. In truth the same thing was in my marriage after I realize that it wasn't going to work I should have taken the necessary steps to end that sooner. It was repetitive. It was comfortable. Sometimes I ask myself, "Why I didn't do this sooner. Why didn't I move to the corporate world? Why didn't I start a business even sooner?" I could have. I look back now and I can see that I was just standing there. Waiting.

Don't just wait. Time keeps going, but so often we find ourselves just marking time, like I mentioned before about walking as though we were on a treadmill—in movement, but not in progression. Busy, but not going anywhere. Yes, I could have done it then. But rather than living in the "used to's and could haves", now I'm just simply glad that I am now where I am. Now my income has tripled. Now I know that I had it in me to succeed. Now I get to encourage women just like you to be in progress and to go get your "Go".

Today Is Your Day

Go Get Your Go!

I know it can be scary. There are so many legitimate excuses that hold us back from going and getting our "Go". Having children, dealing with change can be difficult, feeling like we are older or maybe even 'too old' to begin to make a change. Stuck in a rut. The thing we don't realize is that we have so much more in us. Sometimes we try things and life gives us a reality check. And we think to ourselves, "See, I told you I couldn't do it." We hate to start over. We are comfortable being comfortable. But until we get to a point where being comfortable is no longer an option, change won't happen. It's a challenge to no longer be comfortable. But we have to do that to get to the next level. We have to be uncomfortable to make the progress that we want to make. So today is your day to go get your go.

First off, write down your goals. Again, look at yourself, the full person that you are and decide what you want in every area of your life, physically, mentally, emotionally, and spiritually. Once you've decided your goals, then create an action plan for what you need to do to achieve those goals. Work at those goals consistently and specifically every day.

We have to look at ourselves and realize that the best investment we can make is to invest in ourselves and know that without a doubt, we can do it. You've done it for the company you work for. For the people that you care about and love. If you can do it for the others, then you owe it to yourself to do it for you too. You're a worthwhile investment and now is your time to invest in yourself. I know as you've read this, there have been times when you've been encouraged and inspired. Times when you've been scared. Times when you thought to yourself that maybe it's more than you can take on. But what I know, is that you can do it. It's time to take action. It's time to stop being comfortable. It's never too late as long as you have breath in your body, you have time. Don't wait any longer. Let today be the day that you begin changing. Let today, now, be the day you go get your "Go".

www.ingramcontent.com/pod-product-compliance
Lightning Source LLC
Chambersburg PA
CBHW071244220526
45468CB00002B/1005